A gift for

_____

From

_____

Date

_____

AS SOUTHERN AS IT GETS™

H. JACKSON BROWN, JR.

Published in Nashville, Tennessee, by Thomas Nelson. Thomas Nelson is a registered trademark of HarperCollins Christian Publishing, Inc.

Illustrations by Fred Sayers, sayersf@bellsouth.net
Book design by Bill Kersey at www.kerseygraphics.com

Thomas Nelson titles may be purchased in bulk for educational, business, fund-raising, or sales promotional use. For information, please e-mail SpecialMarkets@ThomasNelson.com.

ISBN: 978-0-7180-9810-0

Printed in China

17 18 19 20 21 DSC 6 5 4 3 2 1

To Bus, Tootie,
Sallye and son, Adam.
Thank you.

Introduction

"Grits in the morning,
grits at night,
grits anytime, anywhere
is a mighty alright."

I tasted grits at age two. They were warm, buttered, sprinkled with sugar, and perfectly prepared by Mother's loving hands. They were impossible to resist then, and I've spent little time resisting them ever since.

I'm reminded of a story attributed to Truman Capote. Seems Truman's New York editor was visiting him at his childhood home in Alabama. Mr. Editor spent the night, and Truman thought he'd show his guest the town the next morning. To get started they stop at a little café on the square for a real southern breakfast. The waitress greets them with a smiling "Good morning, darlins." Truman orders first and asks the New Yorker if he would like some grits with his scrambled eggs and bacon. "Well," Mr. Editor says after giving it some thought, "I think I'll have one." Never having heard of grits, he later confesses he thought it might be some root vegetable the size of a sweet potato. I've always been impressed with the imagination of Yankees.

Now a few comments about this book. If you've noticed, the subtitle is "1071 Reasons to Never Leave the South." I once challenged a tenured professor from one of those Ivy League schools to mirror my efforts and compile a list of "1071 Reasons to Never Leave the North." He heartily agreed and asked me to check with him in a couple of months. After five months, I gave him a call. "How's it going, Professor? How many entries do you have?" He hesitates and mumbles, "Thirty-one." "Would you be so kind to read them," I ask. Well, half were national parks out west, and four entries had something to do with Philly cheese steaks and ice fishing. His embarrassment was my confirmation.

With some confidence I consider myself qualified to offer this list to you. My parents, grandparents, and great-grandparents were born and raised on two hardscrabble farms in Bedford County, Tennessee. So I'm personally acquainted with country ham, smokehouses, mules, canning time, church activities, kudzu, deviled eggs, and one-stoplight towns.

Born in Nashville, Tennessee, I spent my college days at Emory University in Atlanta and then back to Nashville with jobs in music, finance, advertising, film production, and finally some success writing books. I've visited many of the places listed here and enjoyed most of the food. You could say I'm about as southern as a fellow can get and mighty proud of it too.

This list began twelve years ago, and I've had the pleasure of adding to it regularly. In fact, my publisher had to grab it out of my hands two weeks after the deadline. "I need the manuscript today," she commanded. "Just one more day," I pleaded. "I've just thought of three more entries."

The South I love is magical, mysterious, adaptive, independent, proud, historic, but sometimes rough around the edges. The diversity of people, places, and culture; the tears, pride, and promises; the landmarks and landscape; the little towns, country crossroads, and chrome-plated metroplexes make the South a most distinctive region of our great country.

So welcome to my South. Treat her well for she can be very generous. And, as you know, unforgettable.

H. J. B.
Tall Pine Lodge
Fernvale, Tennessee

"Think fast, but speak slowly."

~ HJB

My Favorites

1. cheese grits

2. sweet tea

3. Charlie Daniels

4. the squeak of a rocking chair

5. country ham and red-eye gravy

6. Grand Ole Opry,
   Ryman Auditorium,
   Nashville, Tennessee

7. family reunions

8. grandmother's
   handwritten recipes

9. fried green tomatoes

10. blazes of azaleas

11. the always appropriate remark,
    "Well, bless your heart."

12. coming to the aid of neighbors

13. the evening serenade
    of a mockingbird

14. voracious fondness for pie

15. hymns you know by heart

16. banana pudding

17. shrimp 'n' grits

18. dogwood trees in full bloom

19. deviled eggs

20. checkers played with Coke
    and Pepsi bottle caps

"Southern writers have a great sense of place. That makes you write the truth. When you do that, people read it and say, 'You wrote my life.'"

~ *Maggi Britton Vaughn,*
Tennessee's Poet Laureate
"5 Famous Authors Share
Quotes about the South," *Parade*

Everything Else
from A to Z

22. about everyone you know has
    at least three snake stories

23. acceptance of eccentric relatives

24. accordions

25. Alan Jackson

26. Alan Tate

27. all-day singing and dinner
    on the grounds

28. alligators

29. all-you-can-eat fried catfish
    and hush puppy night

30. "Always on My Mind"

31. "Amazing Grace"

32. ambrosia

33. Amy Grant

34. Andrew Lytle

35. anduille sausage

36. Ann Patchett

37. Anne Rice

38. antique tractor shows

39. anything with a pecan crust

40. apple and peach turnovers

41. Appomattox Court House
    National Historic Park,
    Appomattox, Virginia

forever
Southern

coonhounds

43. apricot preserves

44. Aretha Franklin

45. Arlington National Cemetery, near Washington, D.C.

46. asparagus casserole

47. Atlanta Aquarium, Atlanta, Georgia

48. attending funerals even though you hardly knew the departed

49. Augusta National Golf Course, Augusta, Georgia

50. authenticity

51. **BABY NAMES:** Caroline, Mary Grace, Nathan, Quinn, Savannah, Adelaide, Clementine, Noah, Chloe, Landon, Isabella, Ethan, Abigail

52. backyard vegetable gardens

53. bait shops

54. baked apricots

55. baked sweet potatoes

56. bald eagles

57. baloney sandwiches with a slice of onion and a little mustard

58. banana bread

59. barbeque "bark" crust

60. barbeque restaurants where none of the chairs match

61. barbecued shrimp

62. baskets of ferns hanging on the front porch

63. bass fishing tournaments

66Summer in the deep South is not only a season, a climate, it's a dimension. Floating in it, one must be either proud or submerged.99

~ *Eugene F. Walter*
The Untidy Pilgrim

66Land is the only thing in the world that amounts to anything... 'Tis the only thing in this world that lasts... 'Tis the only thing... worth fighting for—worth dying for.99

~ *Margaret Mitchell*
Gone with the Wind

66. baton twirling contests

67. bay scallops

68. baying of a hound on scent

69. bayous

70. B. B. King and Lucille

71. beachfront cottages named Dream a While, Paradise Dunes, Sandy Toes

72. Beale Street, Memphis, Tennessee

73. beaten biscuits

74. beauty queens

75. beef jerky, deer jerky

76. beignets dusted with
    powdered sugar

77. Bellamy Brothers

78. Benedictine spread

79. Bermuda shorts, madras
    shirts, and Top Siders

forever Southern

dad's
tackle box

81. Bessie Smith

82. Big Mama Thornton

83. Bill Anderson

84. Bill Elliott

85. Bill Monroe

86. bing cherry salad made with Coca-Cola

87. biscuits with sausage gravy

88. Bisquick

89. black beans

90. black bears

91. black iron skillet cornbread

92. black velvet portraits of Elvis

93. blackberry cobbler

94. Blackberry Farm,
    Walland, Tennessee

95. blackberry preserves

96. blackened redfish

97. "Blue Bayou"

98. "Blue Moon of Kentucky"

99. Blue Ridge Parkway,
    North Carolina

100. bluebird houses

101. Bluebird Café,
     Nashville, Tennessee

102. Bobbie Ann Mason

103. Bobby Allison

"Being Southern isn't talking with an accent...or rocking on a porch while drinking sweet tea, or knowing how to tell a good story. It's how you're brought up—with Southerners, family (blood kin or not) is sacred; you respect others and are polite nearly to a fault; you always know your place but are fierce about your beliefs. And food—along with college football—is darn near a religion."

~ *Jan Norris*
Quoted in *Parties and Porches*,
by Brenda Murphy and Friends

105. Bobby Bare

106. Bobby Jones

107. boiled custard

108. boiled peanuts

109. Booker T. Washington National Monument, Hardy, Virginia

110. boot scootin'

111. Booth Western Art Museum, Cartersville, Georgia

112. bottle trees

113. bouillabaisse

114. box suppers

115. bread and butter pickles

116. bread pudding with
     vanilla sauce

117. breezeways

118. Brenda Lee

119. Bristol Motor Speedway,
     Bristol, Tennessee

120. brogans

121. buck dancin'

122. burgoo

123. Busch Gardens, Tampa, Florida

124. "busier than a Memphis
     lawyer on Judgment Day"

125. butter beans

forever
Southern

baby chicks

127. Butterbean Festival,
Pinson, Alabama

128. buttermilk pie

129. butterscotch pie

130. Cajun culture and zydeco
music ("AIEEE")

131. calamine lotion

132. calling elders "Mr." and "Mrs."

133. Calloway Gardens, Pine
Mountain, Georgia

134. camellias

135. candied pecans

136. candied yams

137. caramel cake

138. Carl Perkins

139. Carnton Plantation and Carter House, Franklin, Tennessee

140. Carolina Gold rice

141. Carolina jasmine

142. "Carolina on My Mind"

143. Carrie Underwood

144. carrot cake

145. Carson McCullers

146. cast-iron skillets

147. cat head biscuits

148. *Cat on a Hot Tin Roof*

149. "catawampus"

"Don't compromise yourself — you're all you have."

~ *John Grisham*
The Rainmaker

151. catching fireflies in a Mason jar

152. cedar Christmas trees

153. cedar hope chests

154. cedar whittling sticks

155. chainsaw carving

156. char-grilled oysters

157. Charlie Louvin

158. Charlie Pride

159. Chattanooga Choo Choo,
     Chattanooga, Tennessee

160. Cheekwood Botanical Garden
     and Museum of Art,
     Nashville, Tennessee

161. cheerful clerks greeting you
     with: "Howdy, how are you?
     How can I help you?"

162. cheese straws

163. chenille bedspreads

164. cherry tomatoes stuffed
     with deviled ham

165. chess pie

166. Chet Atkins

167. chicken and dumplings

168. chicken fried in a black
cast-iron skillet

169. chicken-fried steak
with milk gravy

forever
Southern

fence posts
hugged with
honeysuckle vines

171. **ALL SOUTHERNERS KNOW A FEW CHICKEN JOKES:** Q. Why did the chicken cross the road? A. To prove to the possum that it could be done. Q. What happened when the hen ate a bag of cement? A. She laid a sidewalk. Q. Which day of the week do chickens fear most? A. Fry-day. Q. Why does a chicken coop have two doors? A. With four doors it would be a chicken sedan. Q. Why is it easy for chicks to talk? A. Because talk is cheep. Q. What do you get when you cross a chicken with a duck? A. Eggs and quackers. Q. How do baby chickens dance? A. Chick to chick.

172. chicken livers on rice

173. chicken salad

174. chicory coffee

175. chiggers (pound for pound the meanest creatures on earth)

176. chili cook-off festivals

177. chittlins

178. chivalry

179. chocolate cola cake

180. chocolate gravy

181. chow-chow relish

182. Chris Stapleton

183. Christmas at Biltmore, Asheville, North Carolina

184. Chuck Berry

185. church choirs

186. church committee ladies

187. church hand fans advertising the local funeral home

"Try to be a rainbow in someone's cloud."

~ Maya Angelou
Letter to My Daughter

forever Southern

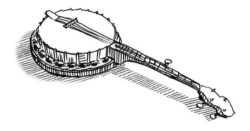

banjos

190. "Church in the Wildwood"

191. church summer camp

192. church women's cookbooks

193. cicadas

194. City Park, New Orleans

195. classic Greek Revival homes

196. Clyde Edgerton

197. Coach Adolph Rupp

198. Coach "Bear" Bryant

199. Coach Dean Smith

200. Coach Ed Temple

201. Coach Mike Krzyzewski

202. "Coat of Many Colors"

203. Coca-Cola cake

204. coconut layer cake

205. cold, baked potato salad

"SEE ROCK CITY"
painted on an old barn roof

207. collard greens

208. college football, "Roll Tide," "War Eagles," "Go Vols," "Hotty Toddy"

209. "come back" sauce

210. comforts of continuity

211. "Company's coming, add a cup of water to the soup."

212. conch fritters

213. concrete yard art

214. Connie Smith

215. considering mac 'n' cheese a vegetable

216. Conway Twitty

217. Cormac McCarthy

218. corn pudding

219. cornbread crumbled in a glass of buttermilk and eaten with an ice tea spoon

220. cornbread dressing

221. corncob jelly

222. country churches'
     Decoration Sunday

223. country fried steak

224. country ham biscuits perfected
     with a dab of orange marmalade

225. Country Music Hall of Fame,
     Nashville, Tennessee

226. county fair pig races

227. courthouse square cafés

66 This is a place where grandmothers hold babies on their laps under the stars and whisper in their ears that the lights in the sky are holes in the floor of heaven. 99

~ *Rick Bragg*
Somebody Told Me

229. courthouse squares

230. courthouse whittlers

231. covered dish suppers

232. crab apple jelly

233. crab boils

234. crab cakes

235. crabmeat sardou

236. Cracker Barrel's cole slaw

237. crawfish boils

238. crawfish jambalaya

239. cream corn

240. creative use of language

241. crepe myrtle

242. crickets chirping, owls
     hooting, frogs croaking

243. cruising Daytona's
     wide white beach

244. cryin' and lonely sound of steel guitars

245. croppie fishing

246. Crystal Bridges Museum of American Art, Bentonville, Arkansas

247. cucumbers and onions (cukes 'n' onions)

248. "cute as a button"

249. cypress knees

250. "Dagnapit!"

forever
Southern

first whiff of
wood smoke from
a mountain cabin

252. Dale Ann Bradley

253. Dale Earnhardt

254. Dale Earnhardt Jr.

255. damson preserves

256. "darker than the inside of a cow"

257. Darlington Raceway,
Darlington, South Carolina

258. Daytona 500, Daytona
Beach, Florida

259. débutantes

260. deep-sea fishing in the Gulf for billfish, blue martin and tarpon

261. Delta blues

262. Delta Blues Museum, Clarksdale, Mississippi

263. demolition derbies

264. Derby pie

265. desserts made with Ritz crackers

266. deviled egg serving plates

267. devotion to duty

268. devotion to family

269. "diddly squat"

270. dirty rice

271. divinity candy

272. "Dixieland Delight"

273. dobros

"I prefer my
oyster fried.
Then I'm sure
my oyster died.**"**

~ Roy Blount Jr.
Save Room for Pie

275. dodging roadkill

276. **DOGS RIDING SHOTGUN IN PICKUPS:** Pokey, Tuna, Jacko, Hot Ticket, Zipper, T-Bone, Hoover, Gitup, Preacher, Sailor, Traveler, Chief, Pot Luck, Tinker, Duebill, Blue, Sarge, Turbo, Ranger, Soot, Jake, Belle, Reload, Delta

277. Dollywood, Pigeon Forge, Tennessee

278. Don Williams

279. "Don't get too big for your britches."

280. double-wides

281. dove season

282. Dr. Pepper (at 10-2-4 o'clock)

283. Dr. Ralph Stanley and the Clinch Mountain Boys

284. draft mules named Dan and John

285. dragonflies

286. *Driving Miss Daisy*

287. driving the truck that
announces your personality

288. dry-rubbed baby back ribs

289. drystone stacked fences

290. dually trucks

291. duck calls

292. "Dueling Banjos"

293. Duke's Mayonnaise

294. dulcimers

forever
Southern

swayin'
front-porch
swings

gourd bird houses

297. Durkee Famous Sauce

298. Earl Scruggs

299. Early Bird Specials,
     4:00 till 5:30 p.m.

300. Eat-A-Snacks opened
     with your teeth

301. eating a perfectly ripe July
     Georgia peach while standing
     over the kitchen sink and letting
     the sweet juice run down your
     arm (This a "Sink Peach.")

302. Eddy Arnold

303. eggnog

304. egrets standing silently
in a lagoon

305. Elvis

306. Elvis impersonators

307. Elvis's Graceland,
Memphis, Tennessee

308. Emmylou Harris

309. end-of-the-dock seafood shacks

66Everybody is
nothing until
you love them.**99**

~ Tennessee Williams
The Rose Tattoo

“I did a lot of writing, writing, writing. The only thing I could think about was Louisiana. The body went to California but the soul remained here.**”**

~ *Ernest Gaines*
WALD News 10 Interview

312. Eric Church

313. Ernest Tubb

314. Everglades National Park, Florida

315. Everly Brothers

316. exploding colors of Atlanta in the spring

317. Expression of commitment: "Long as I've got a biscuit, you've got half."

318. factory outlets

319. families gathered for Sunday dinner after church

320. family Bibles

321. fatback

322. fathers carving the Thanksgiving turkey

323. fiddlers

324. fiddlers' jamborees

325. field peas

forever
Southern

hand-cranked
peach ice cream

66 That sinuous southern life, that oblique and slow and complicated old beauty, that warm thick air and blood warm sea, that place of mists and languor and fragrant richness... 99

~ *Anne Rivers Siddons*
Colony

328. "fields of cotton that spread to the horizon in snowy whiteness"

329. fig preserves

330. filé gumbo

331. first hint of fall

332. flamingos standing proud and flamboyant

333. flip flops

334. flirting

335. Florida Keys

336. Foggy Mountain Boys

337. "Foggy Mountain Breakdown"

338. *Forrest Gump*

339. Fort Sumter
National Monument,
Charleston, South Carolina

340. 4-H Clubs

341. fourth-grade Christmas
pageants

forever
Southern

sleeping
soundly in a
feather bed

343. fox hounds

344. Fox Theater,
Atlanta, Georgia

345. Friday night high school
football under the lights

346. fried chicken and waffles

347. fried chicken livers

348. fried dill pickle slices

349. *Fried Green Tomatoes*
(the book and movie)

350. fried okra

351. fried pork chops (sometimes for breakfast)

352. fried shrimp with cocktail sauce

353. fried soft-shell crabs

354. Frito chili pie

355. frog giggin'

356. frolicking dolphins

357. fruit tea

358. Future Farmers of America

359. Gaither Vocal Band

360. gallantry of Southern men

361. gardenia corsages

362. Garth Brooks

363. Gatlin Brothers

364. gentility of Southern women

forever
Southern

gently
waving
sea oats

366. "Gentle on My Mind"

367. George Jones

368. George Strait

369. Georgia Aquarium, Atlanta, Georgia

370. "Georgia on My Mind"

371. Georgia peaches topped with sweet cream

372. Georgia Sweet Potato Festival, Ocilla, Georgia

373. Georgia's offshore wild horses

374. getting out the good china
when the preacher is
invited to Sunday dinner

375. giblet gravy

376. girls nicknamed "Sista"

377. "gimme some sugar"

378. gimmie caps

379. **GIRLS' DOUBLE FIRST NAMES:** Bonnie Sue, Peggy Sue, Bonnie Jean, Jean Louise, Gloria Jean, Ida Lou, Thelma Lou, Barbara Sue, Thelma Louise, Lilly Mae, Mary Claire, Ella Kay, Bobby Lynn, Sarah Beth, Mary Louise, Anna Mae, Georgia Rose, Olive Jean, Mary Belle

380. giving thanks before meals

381. Glen Campbell

382. gliding formations of pelicans

383. golf cart parades

"Don't give up before the miracle happens."

~ Fannie Flagg
I Still Dream About You

385. *Gone with the Wind* (the book, movie, and movie theme)

386. Goo Goo Clusters

387. gospel quartets

388. **GRANDDAD'S SAYIN'S:** A biscuit ain't a biscuit 'less there's gravy on it"; "happier than a moth in a mitten"; "more annoying than a reunion of Yankees"

389. Grandfather Mountain Highland Games and Gathering O' Scottish Clans, Linville, North Carolina

390. grandmothers in aprons

391. grape jelly meatballs

392. Grapette

393. gravel parking lot at the
American Legion

394. great barbecue debates

395. green bean casseroles made
with cream of mushroom
soup and topped with
French fried onion rings

396. green tomato pickles

397. grilled oysters

398. grilled red fish

399. grouper sandwiches

400. "guitar pulls"

401. gulls resting on pier posts

402. ham hock and black-eyed peas

403. hand fishin' (noodling)

404. hand-crafted dulcimers

forever
Southern

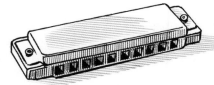

harmonicas

406. **HANDMADE QUILT PATTERNS:** Double Wedding Rings, House on a Hill, Steps to the Altar, Grandmother's Flower Garden, Indian Trail, Old Maid's Puzzle

407. hand-woven sawgrass baskets

408. hand-woven white oak baskets

409. "handier than a pocket on a shirt"

410. Hank Snow

411. Hank Williams

412. "happy as a dog with two tails"

413. Harper Lee's *To Kill a Mockingbird*, the book and movie

414. Harry Connick Jr.

415. Harry Crews

416. harvest festivals

417. Hatch Show Print, Nashville, Tennessee

418. "Haven't seen you in a month of Sundays."

419. having a relative who once worked at Opryland, Nashville, Tennessee

420. hawg-callin' contests

421. head cheese

422. heart of pine plank floors

423. hearts of palm salad

424. *Hee Haw* reruns

425. heirloom tomatoes

66 The blue granite that in some places came up to both sides of the highway; the brilliant red clay banks slightly streaked with purple; and the various crops that made rows of green lace-work on the ground. The trees were full of silver-white sunlight and the meanest of them sparkled. 99

~ *Flannery O'Connor*
A Good Man Is Hard to Find

66I come from down south, where vegetation does not know its place. Honeysuckle can work through cracks in your walls and strangle you while you sleep. Kudzu can completely shroud a house and a car parked in the yard in one growing season.**99**

~ *Bailey White*
Mama Makes Up Her Mind

428. "He's got enough money
to burn a wet mule."

429. hibiscus

430. hidden courtyard gardens in
Savannah and New Orleans

431. High Museum of Art,
Atlanta, Georgia

432. high school cheerleaders

433. high school football

434. high school marching bands

435. Highway 17, South Carolina

436. Highway U.S. 61,
"The Blues Highway"

437. hissy fits

438. historic Carnton Plantation
and Carter House,
Franklin, Tennessee

439. historic Charleston homes
along the Battery

440. hoecakes served with
hot maple syrup

forever
Southern

going barefoot
on the way to
the favorite
swimming hole

442. hog jowl

443. home of Margaret Mitchell, Atlanta, Georgia

444. homecoming dances

445. homecoming queens

446. homegrown Bradley tomatoes

447. homegrown tomatoes sliced and placed between two slices of white bread spread with Miracle Whip

448. hominy

449. hoop cheese and crackers

450. hoop skirts

451. hoppin' John

452. hot browns

453. hot buttermilk biscuits spread with butter and blackberry preserves

454. hot pepper jelly

455. hot pepper vinegar

456. hot water corn cakes

457. Hovie Lister and the Stamps

458. "humidity so bad Sunday didn't get around till late Tuesday morning"

459. Hummingbird cake

460. hummingbirds

461. hydrangeas

462. "I swanney"

66 There's nothing like
5 acres of cotton
and two milk cows
to make a man want
an education. **99**

~ *Ferrol Sams*
Georgia Magazine
February 2007

464. "I Will Always Love You"

465. ice water served in restaurants without your having to ask

466. "I'm So Lonesome I Could Cry"

467. *In The Heat of The Night*

468. influence of grandparents

469. **INGREDIENT INSTRUCTIONS:** "just a smidgin," "a pinch of this and a pinch of that"

470. Iroquois Steeplechase,
     Nashville, Tennessee

471. It's a "clicker" not a
     "remote control."

472. It's a "fillin' station"
     not a "gas station."

473. "It's slicker than an
     oyster on a tile floor."

474. It's true Southerners speak slow.
     Fact is, I once knew a woman
     from Savannah who took two
     minutes to say, "No thank
     you," but it was said politely.

475. Jackson Square, New
     Orleans, Louisiana

476. Jalapeño cornbread muffins

477. jam cake

478. jambalaya

479. James Agee

480. James Brown

481. James Dickey

482. Jason Aldean

forever
Southern

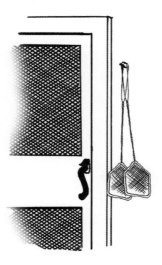

having more than
one flyswatter

484. Jeff Gordon

485. JELL-O salads topped with mayo

486. Jerry Douglas

487. Jerry Reed

488. Jessie Hill Ford

489. jezabel sauce

490. Jim Reeves

491. Jimmie Johnson

492. Jimmy Buffett

493. Jimmy Rogers

494. Joel Chandler Harris

495. Johnny Cash

496. Jon Meacham

497. Juicy Fruit gum

498. Julia Reed

499. June bugs flying on a string

500. Junior Johnson

501. Junior League cookbooks

502. "Just because you were born in the South does not make you a Southerner. After all, if a cat had kittens in the stove, that wouldn't make them biscuits."

503. Justin Timberlake

504. just-picked buttercups displayed in a Mason jar

505. Karo syrup

"We're in the South! We've left the winter! Faint daybreak illuminated green shoots by the side of the road. I took a deep breath; a locomotive howled across the darkness, Mobile-bound. So were we. I took off my shirt and exulted."

~ *Jack Kerouac,*
On the Road

"Treasure the blessings of an average day."

~ HJB

508. Katherine Anne Porter

509. katydids

510. Kay Gibbons

511. keeping family secrets

512. Keith Urban

513. Kennedy Space Center Visitor Complex, Titusville, Florida

514. Kenny Chesney

515. Kentucky Book Fair,
     Frankfort, Kentucky

516. Kentucky Derby,
     Louisville, Kentucky

517. key lime pie

518. Key West sunsets at the
     southernmost point in the U.S.

519. kinfolks waving goodbye
     until you drive out of sight

520. King Cake, Mardi Gras season,
     New Orleans, Louisiana

forever
Southern

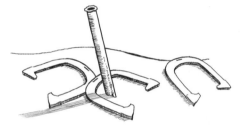

horseshoe
pitchin'

522. King Leo Peppermint Sticks

523. kissin' cousins

524. Kitty Wells

525. "knee-high to a grasshopper"

526. knowing never to ask
what something costs

527. knowing never to wash
a cast-iron skillet

528. knowing someone who worked
as a tour guide at Graceland

529. knowing that cole slaw
sometimes goes on a
barbecue sandwich

530. knowing that going fishing
solves many a problem

531. knowing that outside
clotheslines are strung
north to south

532. knowing the names of
most of your cousins

533. knowing to never
sass your mama

534. knowing to never scare a skunk

535. knowing to never wear an ascot

536. Kris Kristofferson

537. Krispy Kremes

538. Krystal's sliders

539. kudzu

540. Lady Antebellum

541. Lady Baltimore cake

542. Lake Guntersville, Alabama

"Southerners know all too well that a bucket of fried chicken can mean 'I'm sorry,' 'I love you,' or 'Welcome home.'**"**

~ *Johnathon Scott Barrett*
"5 Famous Authors Share Quotes About the South," *Parade*

"'Tell me about where you come from,' a friend once said to me, and I could do no better than this: I love the South because it helps me remember. It helps me know who I am.**"**

~ *Willie Morris*
A Southern Album

545. lanes of moss-draped oaks

546. lard

547. leaning country barns

548. LeAnn Rimes

549. Lee Ann Womack

550. Lee Smith

551. lemon bars

552. lemon chess pie

553. lemon ice box pie

554. Liberty overalls

555. line dancin'

556. Little Big Town

557. Little Jimmy Dickens

558. Liver Mush Festival,
Shelby, North Carolina

559. loblolly pines

560. loggerhead turtles

forever
Southern

lighthouses
silently guarding
the coast

562. "lollygagging"

563. "Lonesome Road Blues"

564. longevity of high
school friendships

565. looking your best when
going to church

566. Lookout Mountain,
Chattanooga, Tennessee

567. Loretta Lynn

568. Louis Armstrong

569. "Louisiana Saturday Night"

570. low country boil

571. low-country marshes

572. "Lucille"

573. Lucinda Williams

574. lunch called dinner and
     dinner called supper

575. Lynyrd Skynyrd

576. Mac Wiseman

577. "mad as five roosters
in a suitcase"

578. "madder than a wet hen"

579. Mae C. Jemison, MD (first
African-American woman
to travel in space, aboard the
space shuttle *Endeavor*)

580. magnificent white blossoms
of giant magnolia trees

581. majorettes

582. mallards

"It's difficult to think anything but pleasant thoughts while eating a homegrown tomato.**"**

~ Lewis Grizzard

584. Manassas National Battlefield, Manassas, Virginia

585. manatees

586. mandolins

587. mangrove islands

588. marble cake

589. Mardi Gras, New Orleans, Louisiana

590. Mark Twain, *Adventures of Huckleberry Finn*

591. marsh grass

592. Martin Luther King Jr. National
Historic Site, Atlanta, Georgia

593. Marty Stuart

594. *Mary Chestnut's Civil
War Journal*, edited by
C. Vann Woodward

595. Mayberry days, Mount
Airy, North Carolina

596. meat 'n' three cafés

597. Memphis barbecue

598. men pulling out chairs for ladies

599. men standing when a
woman enters the room

600. men's seersucker suits
and white buck shoes

601. Merle Haggard

602. mess of greens

603. Michael Shane Neal,
portrait artist

604. Mickey Gilley

forever
Southern

MINOR LEAGUE
BASEBALL TEAMS:

Carolina Mudcats,
Montgomery Biscuits,
Charleston Riverdogs,
Savannah Sand Gnats,
Hickory Crawdads,
Charlotte Stone Crabs,
Macon Peaches,
Columbia Fireflies,
Greensboro Grasshoppers,
Hickory Crawdads

606. midnight shifts at Waffle House

607. mile high biscuits

608. Minnie Pearl "HOW-DEE!"

609. mint tea

610. Miranda Lambert

611. Miss Cantaloupe Queen

612. Miss Catfish Queen

613. Miss Okra Queen

614. Miss Watermelon Queen

615. Mississippi Blues Trail

616. Mississippi Delta's hot tamales

617. Mississippi mud cake

618. Mississippi River steamboats

619. molasses pie

620. monster truck events

621. Monticello, Charlottesville, Virginia

622. Monument Avenue,
Richmond, Virginia

623. Moon Pie Festival,
Bell Buckle, Tennessee

624. Moon Pies

625. Morgan Freeman

626. most anything on a Ritz cracker

627. Mount Vernon,
Mount Vernon, Virginia

628. mountain craftsmen

"Walking the streets of Charleston in the late afternoons of August was like walking through gauze or inhaling damaged silk."

~ *Pat Conroy*
The Lords of Discipline

630. mountain laurel and
rhododendron

631. "moving slow but thinking fast"

632. mud boggin'

633. Muddy Waters

634. muffuletta sandwiches

635. Mule Day,
Columbia, Tennessee

636. muscadine jelly

637. Muscle Shoals Sound,
     Muscle Shoals, Alabama

638. Music Row, Nashville, Tennessee

639. mutton barbeque

640. *My Cousin Vinny*

641. *My Dog Skip*

642. mysterious Everglades

643. NASCAR Hall of Fame,
     Charlotte, North Carolina

644. NASCAR weekends

645. *Nashville* (the movie and TV show)

646. Nashville's Hot Chicken

647. Nat King Cole

648. Natchez Trace Parkway, Tennessee and Mississippi

649. Natchez's Tour of Homes, Mississippi

forever
Southern

Monday wash flappin' on a clothesline

651. National Seashore,
Cumberland Island, Georgia

652. National Storytelling Festival,
Jonesborough, Tennessee

653. National World War II Museum,
New Orleans, Louisiana

654. never substituting
margarine for butter

655. "Never try to out-trade a man
wearing suspenders and a belt."

656. New Orleans' French Quarter

657. **NICKAMES:** Bubba, Bitsie, Junior, Tootie, Bunny, Weezie, Missy, Prissy, Pinky, Rooster, Pepper, Big Dan, Little Bit, Tiny, Bullfrog, Skeet, Speed, Spud, Gopher, Tick

658. no white shoes after Labor Day or before Easter

659. "Nobody eats till we say, Amen!"

660. "noisier than a choir of tomcats"

661. *Norma Rae*

662. North Carolina's Outer Banks

663. "Now, butter my biscuit
and call it done."

664. Oak Alley along Louisiana's
Great River Road

665. Ocoee River whitewater
kayaking in the Cherokee
National Forest, Tennessee
and Georgia

666. okra soup

667. old country stores still
operating as country stores

668. "Old Man River"

"Why is it that no other species but man gets bored? Under the circumstances in which a man gets bored, a dog goes to sleep."

~ *Walker Percy*
Quoted in *Divine Signs*,
by H. L. Goodall Jr.

"You can't run away from trouble. There ain't no place that far.**"**

~ *Joel Chandler Harris*
Uncle Remus

671. older men sitting on their haunches tellin' stories

672. Old-Timey Days Festivals

673. "On the Road Again"

674. "On Top of Old Smokey"

675. one-room schoolhouses now used as community centers

676. open mic songwriter nights

677. Oprah Winfrey

678. Osborne Brothers

679. our Southern drawl

680. our stamina, our pride,
our resourcefulness

681. "our word is our bond"

682. overnight stays in the cabins and
lodge atop Mt. LeConte, Great
Smoky Mountain National Park

683. oyster dressing

684. oyster po'boys

forever
Southern

mournful
train songs

686. oyster-clam chowder

687. oysters Rockefeller

688. palmetto fronds

689. pan-fried quail

690. Panhandle Watermelon Festival, Chipley, Florida

691. paper shell pecans

692. parade of ducks at the Peabody Hotel, Memphis, Tennessee

693. pastel colors of seaside cottages

694. Patsy Cline

695. Patty Loveless

696. Pawleys Island hammocks

697. "Peace in the Valley"

698. peach chutney

699. peach festivals

700. peach pie

701. peach preserves

702. peach salsa

703. peach tea

704. peanut soup

705. pear preserves

706. Pearl Bailey

707. pecan divinity

708. pecan pie

"If you work hard
and you play well,
all those critics
quiet themselves
pretty quickly.**"**

~ Peyton Manning

710. pecan pralines

711. pepper jelly and cream
cheese spread on crackers

712. Peter Taylor

713. photos of grandfathers
in bib overalls

714. Pickapeppa Sauce

715. pickin' and grinnin'

716. picking blackberries while
watching for snakes

717. pickled okra

718. pickled shrimp

719. pig ear sandwiches

720. Piggly Wiggly

721. pimento cheese on crackers

722. pimento cheese sandwiches

723. pimento cheese spread
on a burger

724. pimento cheese stuffed
in celery stalks

725. pineapple upside-down cake

726. pinto beans with
chow-chow relish

727. *Places in the Heart*

728. plantation shutters
softening the light

729. plates of barbequed ribs served
with two slices of plain white
bread and a roll of paper towels

forever
Southern

BEULAH

names of small
towns announced
on water towers

731. playing dominoes

732. playing Old Maid and Rook
with your family at Christmas

733. poke salad

734. pole beans

735. polishing the family silver
before hosting a big event

736. Pop sodas are ordered
as "Co-Cola."

737. porch ceilings painted sky blue

738. porches facing the ocean

739. pork rinds

740. possums

741. pot o' greens

742. potlikker

743. pound cake

744. pouring peanuts in
     your RC Cola

745. power of faith

746. "Precious Memories"

747. Preservation Hall Jazz Band,
New Orleans, Louisiana

748. "prettier than three
brides in June"

749. pride in place

750. prize-winning, handmade baby
clothes exhibited at the state fair

751. prune cake

752. pulled pork barbeque
sandwiches with white sauce

"I remember pimento cheese being the peanut butter of my childhood.**"**

~ *Reynolds Price*
Quoted in *The 2003 Pimento Cheese Invitational*

754. pumpkin pie

755. quilts made by your great-grandmother

756. raccoons

757. radio station WSM's Eddie Stubbs's encyclopedic knowledge of country music, Nashville, Tennessee

758. "Rainy Night in Georgia"

759. Ramp Festivals celebrating the *stinky* ramp throughout southern Appalachia every April and May

760. ramps

761. Randy Travis

762. "Rather push a Chevy than drive a Ford." (comment made by a friend who is a Chevy dealer)

763. Ray Charles

764. Ray Price

765. Ray Stevens

766. Reba McEntire

767. red barns and green tractors

768. red beans and rice

769. red checkered oilcloths
on kitchen tables

770. "Red Dirt Road"

771. Red Grooms

772. red snapper

773. Red Velvet cake

774. redbud trees in the spring

forever
Southern

one-stoplight
towns

776. Reese Witherspoon

777. relatives who play the guitar, fiddle, or banjo really well

778. respect for callused hands

779. respect for police officers

780. respect for teachers

781. respect for tradition

782. restaurant buffet sign: "Take all you want but don't embarrass your Mama."

783. Rhonda Vincent

784. rhubarb pie

785. rice pudding

786. Richard Petty

787. Ricky Skaggs

788. Ridgeway Cantaloupe Festival, Ridgeway, North Carolina

789. riding lawn mower races

790. roadside fireworks stands

791. roadside historical markers

792. roadside pecan stands

793. roadside vegetable stands

794. Robert Leroy Johnson, bluesman

795. Robert Penn Warren

796. Rock City,
Chattanooga, Tennessee

797. "Rocky Top"

798. Roger Miller

66Anyone who
ever gave you
confidence, you
owe them a lot.**99**

~ *Truman Capote*
Breakfast at Tiffany's

"It is a scientific fact that your body will not absorb cholesterol if you take it from another person's plate.**"**

~ *Dave Barry*
Quoted in *Forbe's Book of Quotations,*
edited by Ted Goodman

801. Ron Rash

802. Ronnie Milsap

803. roosters announcing a new day

804. Roy Orbison

805. RV camper shows

806. sacred Indian mounds

807. salt pork

808. saltwater marshes

809. Sam Phillips

810. sand between your toes,
a lost flip-flop, wet bathing
suits, coconut-scented suntan
lotion, a half-finished book,
and an afternoon nap

811. sandpipers

812. Sandra Bullock

813. sassafras tea

814. satsuma oranges that arrive
just before Thanksgiving

offering everyone
who drops
by something
refreshing to drink

816. sausage biscuits spread with
a smidgen of grape jelly

817. Savannah's historic
24 city squares

818. saving bacon grease
for use later on

819. sawmill gravy

820. saying or hearing the
word "Natchitoches"

821. screened-in porches

822. seafood gumbo

823. SeaWorld, Orlando, Florida

824. secretly helping others

825. "See y'all tomorrow if the good Lord's a-willin' and the creek don't rise."

826. seven layer salad

827. "shade tree pick'n'"

828. she-crab soup

829. "She's pretty as a pie supper."

830. sheet cake

831. Shelby Foote's *The Civil War: A Narrative*

832. shells collected during early morning seaside strolls

833. Shenandoah Apple Blossom Festival, Winchester, Virginia

834. Shenandoah National Park, Virginia

835. Shiloh National Military Park near Savannah, Tennessee

66You can't always
be the strongest or
most talented or
most gifted person
in the room, but
you can be the
most competitive.**99**

~ *Coach Pat Summitt*
Reach for the Summit

837. shindigs

838. shoofly pie

839. shopping carts we call "buggies"

840. short summer downpours
at the beach

841. showing respect by pulling over
for a funeral procession to pass

842. shrimp boils

843. shrimp creole with rice

844. shrimp etouffee

845. *Shrouds of Glory* by Winston Groom

846. "Shut the door. Do you think you were born in a barn?"

847. Silver Queen corn

848. "Silver Threads and Golden Needles"

849. sipping the sweet nectar from honeysuckle blossoms

850. sisters singing harmony

851. sitting on the front porch and waving to neighbors

852. skillet-fried frog legs

853. skinny-dipping

854. Skyline Drive (105-mile road running the entire length of Shenandoah National Park, Virginia)

855. sleeping porches

856. sleeping under the sound of rain on a tin roof

forever
Southern

porch lights left on until everyone is safely home

858. Slim Jim snacks

859. slurping oysters on the half-shell

860. small towns' Christmas parades

861. small towns' Fourth
of July parades

862. Smithfield Hams

863. smoked sausage

864. smoked trout

865. *Smokey and the Bandit*

866. "Smoky Mountain Rain"

867. snapping beans on
the front porch

868. snipe hunts

869. "so bowlegged he can't
catch a pig in a ditch"

870. "so poor we'd eat dough for
breakfast and sit outside
in the sun for lunch"

871. soft ocean breezes

872. soft spring rains

873. soft-shell crabs

874. soppin' a biscuit

875. sorgham syrup

876. soul food

877. sound of a screen
door slamming

878. sour cream biscuits

879. sourwood honey

880. souse

❝I am a writer who came
of a sheltered life. A
sheltered life can be
a daring life as well.
For all serious daring
starts from within.**❞**

~ Eudora Welty
One's Writer's Beginnings

882. South Carolina Lowcountry

883. Southern belles

884. Southern historical societies

885. speckled trout

886. spoonbread

887. spoonbills

888. spring onions

889. Spring Pilgrimage Tour,
Natchez, Mississippi

890. square dances

891. squash casserole

892. stacks of *Farmers' Almanacs*

893. "Stars Fell On Alabama"

894. stately antebellum white-columned houses

895. Statesmen Quartet

896. Stephen Ambrose

897. Steve Wariner

898. stick baloney

899. sticky summer nights and
baseball under the lights

900. stock cars racing on dirt tracks

901. stories told so well you'd
think they had a heartbeat

902. strawberries

903. strawberry shortcake

904. Stuckey's pecan log rolls

forever
Southern

"puttin' up" vegetables from the garden in Mason jars

906. Studio B, Nashville, Tennessee

907. stuffed red snapper

908. sugar maple trees in the fall

909. Sun Records Studio,
      Memphis, Tennessee

910. "Sunday Morning
      Coming Down"

911. surf fishing

912. Suwannee River

913. swamps, bogs, and bayous

914. sweet corn on the cob

915. "Sweet Georgia Rain"

916. "Sweet Home Alabama"

917. sweet milk gravy

918. sweet potato biscuits

919. Sweet Potato Festival,
Darlington, South Carolina

920. sweet potato fries

921. sweet potato pie

922. sweet scent of honeysuckle
at twilight

923. Tabasco sauce

924. tailgating before the big game in
the Grove, Oxford, Mississippi

925. taking over homemade soup or
a casserole when someone's sick

926. talented family members
who repair lawn mowers
and train dogs

HOW
TO BE HAPPY

- Pet a dog.
- Call a friend.
- Eat a biscuit.

~ HJB

"She was so Southern
that she cried tears that
came straight from
the Mississippi, and
she always smelled
faintly of cottonwood
and peaches.**"**

~ *Sarah Addison Allen*
Garden Spells

929. tales of pirates and
buried treasure

930. Talladega Superspeedway,
Talladega, Alabama

931. Tammy Wynette

932. tapioca pudding

933. "Tara's Theme" from the
movie *Gone With The Wind*

934. tarpon fishing

935. T-Bone Walker

936. Tennessee Aquarium, Chattanooga, Tennessee

937. Tennessee Pride of the Southland Band, University of Tennessee, Knoxville, Tennessee

938. Tennessee Strawberry Festival, Dayton, Tennessee

939. *The Andy Griffith Show*

940. the arduous Appalachian Trail

941. the band Alabama

forever
Southern

rural
mailboxes
in a row

943. the Blues Hall of Fame,
     Memphis, Tennessee

944. The Carter Family

945. The Cloister, Sea Island, Georgia

946. *The Color Purple*

947. the comfort of culture

948. the culture of bacon

949. "The Dance"

950. The direction: "Not far.
'Tis about two look sees."

951. The excuse: "It's just tradition."

952. the glorious sight of geese in
formation winging south

953. *The Great Santini*

954. The Great Smoky Mountains
National Park

955. The Happy Goodman Family

956. The Hermitage, home of Andrew
Jackson, east of Nashville

957. The Homestead, Hot Springs, Virginia

958. "The House That Built Me"

959. The Imperials

960. The Judds

961. *The Longest Yard*

962. The Martins

963. *The Miracle Worker*

66 When the Bartrams, early horticulturists and adventurers, roamed the South, they were awed by the magnolias. The bloom spells South, primitive and elegant. What other flower is there to lie on the dark wood coffin of your father? 99

~ *Frances Mayes*
Under Magnolia

965. the mist that crowns the
Smoky Mountains

966. The National WWII Museum,
New Orleans, Louisiana

967. The Oak Ridge Boys

968. The Parthenon,
Nashville, Tennessee

969. the philosophy that hard
work will get you places

970. The Ringling Brothers
Circus Museum & Estate,
Sarasota, Florida

971. the romantic-sounding town name "Kissimmee"

972. the sanctity of traditions

973. **THE SOUTH IS KNOWN FOR ITS MILD CLIMATE, BUT, BY JIMINY, IT SOMETIMES GETS HOT:** It's so hot I once saw a dog chasing a cat and they were both walking, It's so hot that birds use potholders to pull worms out of the ground, It's so hot the fire alarm went off in my icemaker, It's so hot snails were hitchhiking, It's so hot my lawn sprinkler took a cold shower, It was so hot I saw two trees chasing the same dog, It's so hot the crawfish are carrying canteens.

974. the spring splendor of Bartlett pear trees in bloom

975. The Statler Brothers

976. the white picket fences of Seaside, Florida

977. The World of Coca-Cola, Atlanta, Georgia

978. thick sliced bacon

979. Thomas Wolfe

980. Thorncrown Chapel, Eureka Springs, Arkansas

forever
Southern

steepled
country
churches

982. thumbprint cookies

983. tidal creeks

984. Tim McGraw

985. Tina Turner

986. tire swing in a side yard

987. Toby Keith

988. Tom T. Hall

989. tomato aspic topped with a
dollop of Duke's Mayonnaise

990. tomato gravy

991. tomato jam

992. tomato pickles

993. tomato pie

994. tomato relish

995. tomato-based barbeque sauce or vinegar-based barbeque sauce (the great debate)

996. "tough as an old pine knot"

997. **TOWNS:** Possum Trot, Kentucky; Toad Suck, Arkansas; Gum Neck, North Carolina; Frostproof, Florida; Monkey's Eyebrow, Kentucky; Bucksnort, Tennessee; Soso, Mississippi; Lickskillet, Tennessee; Two Egg, Florida; Greasy Corner, Arkansas; Bugscuffle, Tennessee; Hot Coffee, Mississippi; Difficult, Tennessee; Lizard Lick, North Carolina; Hog Eye, Arkansas; Loafers Glory, North Carolina; Whynot, Mississippi

998. Trace Adkins

999. tractor pulls

1000. Trisha Yearwood

66It may be that when we no longer know which way to go that we have come to our real journey. The mind that is not baffled is not employed. The impeded stream is the one that sings.99

~ *Wendell Berry*
Standing by Words

1002. "Trust in God but lock the gate"

1003. "trying to find out where
long-passed relatives
buried the silver"

1004. tulip poplar trees

1005. tumbling mountain streams

1006. turnip greens

1007. tutti-frutti cake

1008. Tyler Perry

1009. U.S. Space and Rocket Center,
Huntsville, Alabama

1010. Uncle Dave Macon Days,
Murfreesboro, Tennessee

1011. Universal Studios,
Orlando, Florida

1012. University of Virginia's historic
campus, Charlottesville, Virginia

1013. "useless as a soup sandwich"

1014. Vacation Bible School

1015. vacationing Gatlinburg couples wearing matching T-shirts

1016. The Varsity's chili cheese dogs and onion rings, Atlanta, Georgia

1017. Velveeta

1018. veranda breezes

1019. Victory bib overalls

1020. Vidalia onion jelly

1021. Vidalia onions

cane-pole fishing

1023. Vince Gill

1024. vinegar slaw or creamy slaw

1025. W. C. Hardy

1026. waitresses who greet customers
with "Hon" and "Darlin'" even
though they've never met them

1027. Walt Disney World,
Orlando, Florida

1028. warm, fresh peach cobbler

1029. watermelon seed spittin' contests

1030. Wausau Possum Festival, Wausau, Florida

1031. watermelons (plug them to see if they're ripe)

1032. watermelon-rind pickles

1033. W. E. B. Du Bois

1034. weddings with lots of flower girls and attendants

1035. weekend flea markets

1036. well-cared-for cemeteries

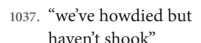

1037. "we've howdied but
haven't shook"

1038. "When in doubt, add
a bit more butter."

1039. where brides wear their
grandmother's pearls

1040. where everyone gets a bit
misty-eyed when describing
the home they grew up in
as "the old homeplace"

1041. where it's okay to say,
"Merry Christmas"

66 You can call us rednecks
if you want. We're not
offended, 'cause we
know what we're all
about. We get up and
go to work, we get up
and go to church, and
we get up and go to
war when necessary. 99

~ *Jeff Foxworthy*
2007 CMT Awards

"A mule will labor
ten years willingly
and patiently for you,
for the privilege of
kicking you once."

~ *William Faulkner*
Sartoris

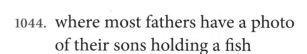
1044. where most fathers have a photo
of their sons holding a fish

1045. "Where they live ain't the
end of the world, but you
can see it from there."

1046. where "yes sir" and "yes
ma'am" are standard replies
to anyone older than you

1047. white bean and ham soup

1048. white ibis

1049. white-tailed deer

1050. wicker porch furniture

1051. "Wildwood Flower"

1052. Will Campbell

1053. "Will the Circle Be Unbroken"

1054. William Gay

1055. Williamsburg Historic District, Williamsburg, Virginia

1056. Wilma Rudolph

forever
Southern

proudly
displaying
Old Glory

1058. wilted lettuce with hot
bacon dressing

1059. windswept barrier islands

1060. wire cricket cages

1061. wisdom of our elders

1062. wisteria climbing a garden trellis

1063. "Won't ya come in
and sit a spell?"

1064. woolly worms

1065. world's biggest catfish fry,
     Paris, Tennessee

1066. Wright Brothers
     National Memorial,
     Kill Devil Hills, North Carolina

1067. "'Y'all' is plural and singular"

1068. You don't "turn off the lights,"
     you "cut off the lights."

1069. Zac Brown Band

1070. zucchini bread

"You'll never do a whole lot unless you're brave enough to try."

~ Dolly Parton
@DollyParton 12 June 2013

And now, a quiet benediction:

To all who have read this far,
"Thank you kindly."

 Your Favorites

Dear Reader,

You've just read my Southern favorites, but I bet I didn't mention many of yours. I'd be pleased to hear from you and learn what I missed. You can reach me at: instructionbook@aol.com

Reader's Favorites

_____

_____

_____

_____

_____

_____

_____

_____

_____

_____

_____